THE
RETURN
TO
SOURCE

A Spiritual Awakening to the
Dark Reality on Earth

JEFF ILSCHNER

Copyright © 2021 Jeff Ilschner
All rights reserved
First Edition

NEWMAN SPRINGS PUBLISHING
320 Broad Street
Red Bank, NJ 07701

First originally published by Newman
Springs Publishing 2021

ISBN 978-1-63692-884-5 (Paperback)
ISBN 978-1-63692-885-2 (Digital)

Printed in the United States of America

To Jolanda

This book is not for providing you proof. It is for opening a doorway in your mind for you to think for yourself and find the proof within you.

Chapter 1

THE MODERNIZED WORLD

Humans living under the modernized world is the reason why they have continued to fail, existing only as a physical race and not a spiritual one. The people living focused only on the modern world, which is why they do not see or know anything with a higher form of self. The whole time, they are thinking it's just normal life when, in fact, it's not; it is the complete opposite. We change our existence in reality through the spirit which comes from within us. Humans understand very little about this process which is a vital part of understanding reality. You cannot spiritually invest in physical success. The spiritual world does not have any ties with the material senses of the living, and trying to tie spiritual focus into a life of modernized success is nothing more than a fantasy illusion of an earthly minded person. Coming into the nature of the living spirit is a return to having the gift of eternal life. The soul and love are truly the same as the soul is made of light and light is love in its purest form. The longer you support your illusions of life, the more you will lose yourself. If you live in fear under this world, the physical body and mind will respond by adopting the functions of the fearful state in reality. The soul heals and brings the mortal presence back into balance with divine form in connection to the source. You must reconnect with the source through the soul to heal pain, suffering, and lost connection to your higher self.

If the people are always only thinking outside with themselves, they will always only look at the exterior side of life, and this will not get them where they need to be. Every individual must search deep within to come into the state of higher existence. Many are blocked right now from receiving any type of higher shifting energy flow, and they must figure out what it is in their lifestyles that is holding them back. Letting go of the modernized world completely is the key to escaping the deceptions of this false reality and finding the universe outside. The physical body is just the vessel that the spirit dwells in giving it life. When the soul is empowered, this changes the physical body, influencing it with the best care in life. The system is designed for controlling the living, keeping people trapped inside their illusions of life, and holding them back in reality from reaching a level with ascension. A person will perceive the reality of what their mind receives. When you take that individual and place them into a system with manufactured authority being processed since birth under gradual indoctrination, this takes them completely out of their state of natural balance, and they have become molded into a whole different person other than who they really are. Instead of standing out in their true form of identity with their inner light shining, they are forced to fit in with the rest of society with their light closed off, all designed to lead the person to lower their self into giving their power to an outside source for control over their entire existence. In the system, everything is used as a distraction to keep the people caught up in mindless physical world affairs so that their attention of focus will allow their energy to flow constantly to the bread and circus acts instead of within themselves which is most important with everyday life for soul growth.

All humans must put self before everything else—before money, before jobs, before daily lifestyles, before house and cars, and even family and friends. The fact that they put everything else first outside of themselves, always giving their energy to other physical sources, is the whole reason as to why they have no true inner power. This is why they have not found their true identity in self for the pathway of the journey. The only way to begin this path is by putting self over everything but still surviving in the world only because, as a necessary function, we must live by and nothing ever more than that. The soul powers the physical body with everything needed for life, but the souls of the people have been conquered with power of control through the powers of this world ruling over them which takes all source of self-identity out of the people. They have given their natural power to that outside source for control with every moment of their existence. Their source of inner light, which is their power, is not in the higher state it should be for them to be in their true living nature they were created for. The identity of every person is not the physical form. The physical presence is just a vessel that the real source of life dwells in whether being of light or shadow. In this world, they have taken almost all light of the soul out of a majority of the people and have them living outside of themselves with the physical existence, but this is not who they really are. The people must come to find this life source inside of them, which is their true identity, and go back to the nature of this in order to live and grow in spiritual form through the light of the soul which powers the heart and mind with divine form. This changes not only their reality but also changes others around them as well. You change yourself; you change others.

CHAPTER 2

FAKE REALITY

Most of this world's population thinks systematically, putting their life force into the system for trusting, always following, and believing it to actually be real instead of putting their aim into self where all truth, love, and wisdom comes from. This is why the physical reality is all the people see for what they know, having no real sense of direction on the right path to come into inner peace for spiritual ascension work. The soul is the highest form of energy where life's true meaning lies for building happiness around. Everything else in this world is an illusion. Humans already contain the light within themselves for learning, but they don't allow them to come into knowing this because the system makes them conditioned to follow other things that are meaningless distractions for holding the people back from reaching their power in real self. This world's system is like a virus. It destroys what humans have inside of them, making them lose access to spiritual information that they had the ability to gain in the beginning before their indoctrination process began at an early age. Education is just the beginning; and one of many ways, they destroy the connection to self, leaving the person with no sense of real identity. As an adult, jobs and having to make money is an overall distraction, causing billions to lose the ability to focus the right thoughts and discover what the human race can really do in reaching its full potential. Your day job you consider to be your career is not your real job. It is an illusion of the enslavement system created for control over your existence to live.

The soul is the greatest source for consciousness which drives us into thinking, acting, and living in ways that lead us on the path to reaching our higher form of self. When people begin to live through the soul, their lives begin to transform. Soul consciousness connects the heart and mind, filling the person with positive life. When a person is in course with the soul, this is the purest way to live. The world in reality shifts, as the light of the soul increases, all behavior as the person becomes more loving and peaceful as the soul is leading them in functional living. This is what brings humans closer to their true nature. Through the soul, we are all loving and peaceful beings. The awakening, healing, and transformation the world needs are in each and every human through the soul; but where are the souls of the people at? They have taken the light out and made men's and women's DNA to become dark in expression, living in lower states of reality and cold and emotionless toward themselves and each other. People having no clear idea what the truth is of this world is because they have been conditioned to live under the physical senses' reality for what they choose to believe and follow with life. The mind does not free the person from the prison of this reality; it is weak with having limited use. Only the soul can free the individual by guiding them on the right passage through the heart and mind. The soul is the source of light which is life in its perfect form, an energy that manifests and directs our journey with living which draws the heart and mind into higher self. The soul powers the physical body with an absolute state of health flowing through every cell in the body. The cells can be so charged that they become as radiant light. More importantly, higher sense, thoughts, and feelings are influenced through the spirit which creates a life with the source of creation to progress in and generate ultimate power in guiding the individual to become pure. Only the pure who have taken back their source of inner power and reclaiming the light of the soul, can develop a direction of spiritual insight into the design of the living body. To understand that which was, you must first understand that which is. So in point, it's not any meaning of discovering anything new but rather coming into knowing what was always there through self-awareness. Now you can understand why they have used everything to take the light out of all people in order to disconnect the living person from their soul, leaving them with little to no chance of coming into grasp with realizing what is truly so. This keeps the population trapped in the material body form in this world until they come to make the changes necessary for a return to their original state of higher being. The more you become informed, the more you alter your reality and others around you as well. Information is light; light is information. How you carry yourself in life is what you broadcast as your frequency to everyone else. The key is focus. If the people can create a higher sense thought outside of society, the planet will shift. For the longest now, they have corrupted and controlled the people, directing their flow of energy in attention on the scripted states of managed chaos staged to produce calm submission through a fear-based reality.

The constant rehashing with the political and religious shows and traumatic events with images of despair and destruction repeatedly implanted into the minds of the viewers creates extreme anxiety through psychological warfare. If you stop watching television programming, especially networks, you are disconnecting yourself from the chaos, anxiety, stress, hustle with money, and temptations of all types that you do not need. You begin to clear and see reality for what it truly is. You start to listen, feel, and know what is going on inside of yourself, living in the world but no longer modernized and lost in it like before. If you rely upon the physical senses for your path, then you are living an extremely confined existence. This is a limited perspective that keeps humans trapped in physical reincarnation through many lives until they have mastered the element of the soul's spiritual ascension process in this dimensional plane. By becoming aware in a state of knowing your sense of spirit, you can expand to strengthen your physical life and soul growth which creates your experience in this physical world's reality, bringing you fully to an awakened state.

CHAPTER 3

HUMAN EVOLUTION

Self is the spiritual aspect of life with human evolution, a state of elevated cognizance and perception through higher consciousness, bringing a person into a deeper understanding of nature and reality. Escaping the cage over the mind that the system has put over everyone with false illusions through society begins the activation of the spiritual senses which you recognize more and listen to for guiding you in the right direction of the journey with your soul's purpose. Humans are here for helping each other, not the system itself. If every human quit their job today and lost everything, they would be better off 'cause they still have each other. The majority of people are caught up with strictly focusing on too much with the physical senses in life, always paying bills and putting food on the table when they really should be more concerned with food for the soul. Too many people chase money and materialism. You don't need money, a house, or a car to be in self; all you need is your soul, the true design of identity. They push materialism at an all-time high now to try and keep the people trapped living under those illusions created for holding them back from reaching any level of ascension which is a higher state of mental and physical being. They know, once the people reach a state of spiritual consciousness, the veil is lifted from over the mind; and they begin to see with the eyes what is factual. Imagine a higher state of self so deep that it produces a much-different life force than you have ever known before. This energy makes you go so high in frequency it is almost an energy felt that is too strong for any mortal body to contain. This flow of life makes you full and complete inside with everything you need for life, and once you have an experience of how this feels, you will fight to keep yourself in this state of being.

Now imagine that this is the exact opposite of what they are and have been purposely teaching humans in this world—race propaganda for more divide and conquer, panic in the streets from the staged attacks, chaotic weather patterns, and political and religious shows for bringing full police hour. They are teaching the people to feed on fear and anger, which lowers them into a level for evil to consume them. These powers of the air work through frequency. Everything is through energy, good and bad and light and dark. People must learn to control their own life force and stop with giving it to the wrong things. Humans are strong, smart, and more powerful than they've been led to believe. If they could wake up and see they are the balance created here from out of the light and could do so much to stop wickedness from destroying the natural world. Power comes from an enlightened person out to change others around, and power adds up in numbers 'cause numbers in high equals strong energy, which becomes ultimate power in this dimension for change. Heightened energy is the greatest weapon against darkness. There is nothing it can do to fight or hide against this; all is revealed to the people more every day, growing more connected into the source itself.

Energy of every individual is important. Learn energy, and you will know the types of people you want to have around you and the ones you want to avoid at all costs. Matching your frequency to those in this world who are of the same level of frequency is the best way for staying high and remaining balanced. Humans have no idea how amazing the energy of the light feels. If, for just half a second of their life, they felt this energy to come over them, they would forget about everything in their modernized mortal life and want only this energy always. Detachment from the physical world is attachment to the spiritual. What is most important lies within the mind, body, and, most importantly, the soul. The thoughts of the mind are driven by the soul through the heart. The heart generates its energy field from the soul. If the soul is strong, then the heart is strong, bringing sharpness to the mind. But if the person is not living through the soul, then the heart is cold, and the mind is closed off, leaving the person to exist strictly in the wickedness of the physical side of life. The majority holds to the belief that power is in the physical, and that is not the case. All true power can only come through the spiritual side with connection to the light of the soul which is the source of power with creation. The people must start now to focus on what matters most, and that lies within themselves. If the light of the human is destroyed from within, then the soul is gone for good, and their existence is dead forever. People have to shift their focus with priorities around and do what is needed in order to make the necessary development. Putting the physical body's needs first before the soul is like putting the cart before the horse. It is the opposite of how it should be, and that is how humans are with everything in life. Physical death should not be feared 'cause physical death is only temporary. Death of the soul is forever, which should be feared the most. The soul is the strongest part of existence. The soul of the damned is dead forever, but the soul of the righteous is eternal and divine.

Without your soul, you would not be in existence. So every time they take more of the spirit out of the people, their life is taken away, and they are brought closer to an eternal death. Society was structured to take the life out of a person, not build it up. The soul is the real identity to come into life in the physical, for being on earth is an experience to find purpose. For one to find the true meaning of purpose with existence is to find the true meaning with life. Only natural life experience can bring a person into finding true meaning of purpose, and purpose can only be found by living through the soul. The people have not found the purpose of their own soul because they have lost the union of the spirit by living under a manufactured reality which is an illusion of grand schemes to keep the people disconnected from finding the purpose of their own soul. It was designed to steal the light of the soul out of all humans and make them strictly physical in nature, having no passage to the purpose of life. The soul is what is important, and you must feed the soul through the physical existence in order to grow the physical existence into spiritual form through the soul. In this world, you cannot be strong in one without the other. People have to want more than what this world has to offer, and if they come to this point of reaching, the soul will open the path to eternal life. The physical body is connected to this world in the dimension the soul is connected to the source, and this is why they have detached humans from their soul in order to keep them held down in mortal form to this prison-planet matrix. Nothing in this world is more important than life itself, and everything they have the people involved with only pertains to death and destruction. Those whose primary focus is to function in the world will never understand. They live under the system; therefore, that is all they will see and know for their reality.

CHAPTER 4

ILLUSIONS OF LIFE

People focus too much on jobs and money. If humans were in control of the system with living, it would be different, but they're not. Everything in life the people live under is a lie. Working a job for money is enslavement. People should be ashamed of what they have been led to become in the path of this nature. People are consumed with establishing themselves in the physical reality and, because of this, have lost all touch with the spiritual reality which is most important. Money is an overall distraction and has absolutely no beneficial value in any person's life other than the continuation of staying physically trapped in a manufactured setting. Most people are afraid to lose their illusions of life when it comes down to that. Free will has been shifted into a way of being viewed as selfish. Those who dare to stand out from the rest of the modernized crowd are judged as outsiders and troublemakers who are mad in the head 'cause they are not like the rest who live under and obey the system. The people of this world have no idea 'cause they are controlled to be ignorant, which brings chaos, never knowledge. Those who take part in the wickedness of society will be devoured by all of the evil it carries with it. You will never find what is right outside through the system. You will always only see and follow what is wrong. A person can only find what is truly right within themselves. People don't know peace 'cause they are not in the spirit. Humans have to want more to life. They have to search within for purpose and stop looking to the outside world for how it wants them to be. The purpose for the living is life itself. But society is not life, and the masses are being distracted, wasting days of their lives away and only helping contribute to the wickedness which holds them back from coming into the essence of the living spirit.

People have to pull their priorities out of the world and get their heads in the game. Your lives are meaningless if you are solely focused on your illusions of life; and all of life, as you know it, is an illusion. There is no accepting any of it. Your jobs, your house, your car, your bills, and all aspects of being a citizen are fake. None of it is real, nor does it matter. If people do not wake up, they will only remain on the path they have been to, becoming worse in every way, looks, emotions, and total existence. The reality that you live in is what you take on in mental and physical form. This is why most of the world looks and feels terrible 'cause they are following a wicked design that was built for their own destruction. All people have to wake up to coming into knowing these things. Nobody is going to do this for you. You have a mind; use it and think for yourself. Otherwise, they're only going to keep heavily conditioning you on what you should think, feel, say, and do. With all of the people conditioned to think and act the same in the world, it is no wonder why nobody gets it or sees anything for understanding. How could they even remotely have any kind of clue when they follow the system in full or in some form or fashion, being guided in its ways, trusting, and believing? The more you understand, the less they will control you. The problem is that people have been conditioned to view information as a conspiracy, and this places the person in a reality with questioning outside of themselves as to whether something is real or in fact true. All truth comes from within; it is never found through any outside source. People debate with others and compare information of different sorts to try and figure out some kind of truth with matters, but it does not work like that.

If you support any part of the system, you are not in control of your own existence because you are still living under your illusions of life, believing that you are actually free when you are not free at all; it is the complete opposite—you are just a slave in a manufactured reality built for control. The main goal is to destroy the people's right to free will on the planet. Once this has been done, full power is reached for control over all of the living. The more people listen to the lies, the more power they have, and the closer they are to reaching that goal. People do not want to listen 'cause they have been conditioned to be ignorant in living under the system. This is why that is all they see and know for their reality with following without the veil being lifted. Reality is what you make it, and if you choose to go that path, you will deal with what it consists of. Nobody is here to show you proof to make you believe anything. A person must find the proof inside. That is the only way the eyes can be opened—through the soul—to see what is real. The mind controls thought reality and will function by what it knows and follows. You have to open the doorway in your life to walk through and make the necessary changes to begin the path to seeing. A lot of people do not want to listen because they are too busy feeling low from how society has gone. They let the system get their emotions with control, and that is exactly what it was designed to do. People must come to a better point of focusing on going deeper than they are with what they think they know. That is the only way that you will see truth in the right mental form. We live in a reality where people believe that truth is found on the Internet; and they base all of their thoughts, words, and actions from there. That is far from being an accurate case. Nobody else is going to think for you. You must do that for yourself, and if you cannot do that, then you need to take a hard look at your life and make the changes needed in order to get there.

Is your physical existence in control, or is your spirit in control? The material body will always have different thoughts and needs than the soul. Think for yourself. You do not need any outside practices or fol-lowings in order to do this. All knowledge is contained within the light of the soul. It's only when people are following in the ways of the world that they become lost and have no sense of direction for the right way on the path of the journey. Patience is strength. The soul is power. Patience can only come from the soul which is eternal. With patience comes understanding. Having understanding brings knowledge. Ultimate freedom can only come through the soul. This is why they designed a manufactured reality to keep people trapped in the physical sense of life so they cannot live in spirit but rather in the nature of the material body. Do people really need the tangible lifestyles of the world, or do they need each other? If, at the end of the day, the people lost every material thing in the world, they would still be fine 'cause they have each other. The soul heals all sides of life. Healing comes from life force energy which is the purest form of love.

Love is the primary force in the manifestation of renewing a person's transformation of inner self, the highest form of existence there is. The soul is the power that spiritually influences a transformation in people around us when we are living in a higher manner of enlightenment with standing out as the true identity of the soul. People have lost sight of this 'cause they have been programmed to function otherwise, fitting in a worldly fashion for being conditioned to be controlled all as one in the physical existence instead of reshaping their presence for prospering in the spirit of inner being. They have conditioned people to not be happy unless they have money, which is an illusion of life. If you cannot be happy without money, then you are not free and are living confined within the prison-state reality in place over the mind, body, and, most importantly, the soul.

Only the soul itself is lasting eternal and purifies the physical existence with everything needed in life. The soul is what powers the physical person with good, clean living. Living strictly in the physical will only lead to a spiritual death. If the people were being led by their spirit, this would guide them into seeing and knowing what is really going on and needing to be done to stop so much of what is bad happening in the world. The human individual must come into knowing that they are enough and way more in self than they could ever imagine in this world that they could be. The light of the soul is eternal power which is never ending. We are energy beings here in the physical. The soul gives form to the presence of the living experience. The physical body is just that—a vessel. If we are living modernized, then we are living in the material form and not in the sense of who we really are. If we are living in the spirit, then we are in the essence of true form and know our real, true nature of existence. The only way to avoid becoming broken as a physical vessel in this structured prison is to be in the spirit. The soul is immortal and the strongest form of everlasting light made eternal. To be in the spirit is to truly know self, and having separated the spirit from the physical form, the true identity of the person is always in control with knowing. Reality is a prison. Only your soul can set you free. Money was designed to make a person become soulless through materialism which detaches the individual from connection with the spirit, making them to only have a physical existence. This keeps the population trapped in the material body form in this world until they come to make the adjustments necessary to make the return to their original state of higher being.

CHAPTER 5

MONEY IS THE ROOT

Money is the basis for the system. All currencies are for humans to pay for living on this planet through enslavement no matter whether it is cash or soon-to-come electronic currencies. Money and credit are nothing more than necessary evils to function living under this world's system that do absolutely nothing beneficial for empowering the life force of the soul itself. The things that are important, you cannot obtain with all the money in this world. What they teach in schools, colleges, and universities is propaganda. Children grow up to be adults that are systematically programmed. The forty-hour work week is a waste of measure with days being a major distraction to keep humans caught up with mindless enslavement to retain their focus off of themselves and away from their true important purpose which is enlightenment for soul growth. What is more for the people? Their repetitive connection with chasing money and the material world, or their one-stop connection with infinite balance through the soul for empowering the life existence with everlasting joy and happiness? If you are living a processed life in the world, you will only see the physical reality and believe everything in society within the global system to be considered normal with life.

Only when you are fully focused getting rid of toxic people, places, and things from your life living outside of it all through the spirit with a higher focus does the veil of illusions disappear from over you; and everything is revealed in the world for the true form of wickedness showing what it really is before the people. To escape this prison-planet reality, you have two things you must be in. One, live physically good and clean with daily lifestyles. No smoking weed, popping pills, using medications, drinking alcohols, or consuming processed foods, just to name a few. Two, you must be awake to everything. A lot of people think they are consciously awake but really are not 'cause they are selective with what truths they choose to believe and follow. It does not work like that. The person must be on the level with everything, not just what they find for convenient, easy truth; and with that being said, the spiritual sense through the soul is the way. You cannot come to know the hidden knowledge of the universe living through the outside of your physical existence in the world.

All knowledge comes from within, and you must seek out your own soul for the answers to life's journey. They hate when a person has total control and carries their character in a higher balanced manner. They get their power from control over people which takes self-focus of the person away whether it's in the workplace, public, or family setting. Having a higher focus eliminates all bad vibration with fears and lowers emotional thoughts and feelings. Once a person has this perfect flow of balance with every moment of life, the system and those who operate and control it have no answer for the individual who is stronger than they are, and this bothers them, not having any control or answer for the level of life force energy they feel coming from the person which affects them. The real self is dangerous. Dangerous for the established system. Dangerous for the church and state. Dangerous for the modernized traditions. Because once a person knows real self, they have become an individual who stands out in this world, no longer fitting in like the rest of the herd-mentality-carrying crowd that are blindly controlled.

All the money in this world will not buy you a path in journey to the soul. The best things in life are free. When you begin the journey to find the ultimate connection to the source, you will lose everything in this world—friends, family, and lifestyles. The old world you knew will go away, and you will find yourself changing in every way within life. You are guided and carried as you continuously make progress, but the journey is not easy. You will not want to be around negative people, places, and things because the veil of negative life has lifted and you see and feel things around you for how the true nature really is. You will spend a lot of moments alone to remain high and charged, working always on yourself to grow more every day, not allowing anything of lower vibration to come and steal any of your focused energy flow for holding you back or slowing you down.

It is at this moment in life that you realize how amazing the process is; and you will not allow anything to come first before this—not job, not money, not toxic people, nor lifestyles anymore. You are now putting your soul first; and nothing compares to or even comes close to being as beautiful and wholesome as the way the light of your soul fills your existence with everlasting love, understanding, and inner peace. You continue to put your attention into people, places, and things that are dead sources for having absolutely no energy in them, only taking yours while you get nothing back in return, always feeling empty with no understanding as to why. It's all about whom and what you are guiding your flow of life to. Your lives are basically meaningless if you are living controlled under the system of this world. Through the power of the soul in self, once you are free of the mental control of this fake reality you are living enslaved under, you cannot imagine how much you do not need anything else but the source itself which is in you with joy, happiness, understanding, and love. The goal of humans on earth is soul evolution whether they realize it or not. Rising above the fear-based reality emotions, learning how to express unconditional love will raise the planetary vibrational levels of each and every individual person, moving closer to a state of harmony filled with joy and happiness. If it seems like a lot of the time you are stuck, not moving, just know that everything is always a state of work in progress, learning the way in life through the energy of works. This is why humans have reincarnated lives for evolving spiritually.

If you are focused solely on fitting in like a citizen with the rest of modernized society, congratulations, you're doing it all wrong with life. The mass majority are blinded to see this with their own faults in the poor choices they have made for choosing to give their life energy to the system which brings all forms of control. Everything in this world within society is a manufactured illusion; none of it is real. But ninety-nine percent of the population holds to the belief that this is actual life, and that is where the problem lies at with their incompetent failure to understand which is why they have failed as a race. You cannot pick and choose as to what you believe to be real or in fact true. You cannot regard one part of society to be fake but accept another part of it as being real just because it resides with you in some form of life fashion that you have become adapted to so much. If you cannot come to a conscious focus of terms that this world is one big illusion of lies, then you are done, and they have you right where they want you.

Wake up and think for yourself. What is most important: sacrificing the people for the growth of the system, or sacrificing the system for the growth of the people? Materialism is in complete control of the economic structure. The individual has been conditioned into becoming a part of the system, providing an economic security at the expense of their human mind, body, and soul. Unless it is coming from nature in a natural setting, everything else—from technology, money, fashion, entertainment, and society as a whole—is a created illusion. The people already had a strong source of life in them long ago. That has been taken out, and they now have a structured process in them which has led to genetic alterations of the entire human genome.

This makes them to become strictly physical in nature, being unnatural and going against everything the intended design of the universe is about. Society is manufactured and fake. When a person is consumed with living in its ways, this destroys the natural life process of the physical existence. The whole reason why people get sick and carry diseases, both physical and mental, is having no inner connection with actual life in this world through a processed system of constructed ages. Wake up! Stop giving your life force to the system and begin to focus it on yourself inside with spiritual ascension to grow your mind, body, and soul as one with the universe. Until you start this process, you will always get what you've had coming. If you are asking "Why is this world this way?" or "What is happening with the world?" you are not paying attention to the right things. As the agenda of the world order progresses in stages, it is only getting worse with each passing year. The current state is in a movement of final phases of exiting the old world order and entering the new world order. Everything they have control over, and humans have allowed to continue with every passing day is another step closer to their victory with destroying everything natural here on this earth. Predictive programming is mind control used as a subtle form of psychological human conditioning provided heavily by the vast media outlets to acquaint the public with planned societal changes that are implemented by the new world order. When these changes are put in place, the people are already familiar with them and have accepted them as the new normal in social progression. These are more laws and regulations for control ran on the unsuspecting public as preemptive mass manipulation.

CHAPTER 6

ILLUSION OF CHOICES

Through the illusion of choices with all views in life, they keep the masses of people divided into camps, making it easier to keep them conquered and under an influence to direct them into fighting with themselves and each other violently over pointless staged political acts rather than finding the source of their true identity and helping their race to rise above the wickedness in this world which works to destroy them. When the people are fighting against evil, it is different with the flow of energy in this manner; but when they are deceived and fighting for evil, being controlled by it through acts of wickedness, this puts them in a whole different type of reality with their essence. Lies are a necessity. They are the source of meaning with hope and belief. The true makers of America founded and built this fake reality on the illusion of choices with politics for division. Politics is the illusion of fake opposition for the people to follow the propaganda of science in politicalism, feeding the people the great lie that they have public figures who are looking out for their best interests in life. Through political engineering in society, institutions were established in place for designing paper decrees in the form of laws, referendums, and ordinances to achieve a desired effect with pushing the people in a certain direction. Civil divide and conquer is the reason for the very founding of the American world order from the start to advance the concept of civil conflict and push forward with their progress, moving right into the new global governance. The beginning of the American era in 1776 was about the founding of the American world order, which is the current global order of power now that we are seeing to be dismantled. We are at the end of this point, and America's time with holding the power of world order is finished. Every age, an empire has risen to fall and usher in the next. We are at the start of another age to begin.

America in itself has always been part of the veil of illusions and was never real. Only the people themselves are real. It was founded on occult beliefs with an intended purpose for having a secret destiny. It always costs lives to bring changes to the world. This is the philanthropy of their world-order agenda. Their plan has always worked through uniting the people as one. There can be no unity without the loss of lives. The greater the common suffering, the greater the false peace. As they drive humanity deeper into its own self-destruction, the same ones who are manufacturing the chaos to bring new order are the same ones who will bring false peace, claiming to have saved humanity from itself. Their system works through a vast network basis involving two ideological formats: political programs and various religious teachings both used heavily on the masses for domination and control over the human mind, body, and soul. Problem-reaction-solution is a mass mental-control method used to make changes to laws that the citizens would never accept otherwise. They create the problem with terrorism, viral outbreaks, financial crisis, and climatic disasters to provoke loss, fear, and outrage. Then they manufacture the reaction, letting the shock of the public to be channeled solely through the mainstream media broadcasting the side of the problem they want to show, promoted for the people to willingly and unquestionably accept their solution which, of course, is the original goal that the public would have never gone along with in the absence of the problem they created. Majority of all people follow the concepts of the false illusion in this world. Not everyone will come to understand much of what is to be learned besides what they see and know coming from the base reality of this system.

The prison-planet matrix works through the life force of soul energy feeding darkness within the agenda, which gives power over the people, taking away their source and self-identity being replaced with rule through enslavement. If the people wake up and come to return in finding to the nature of who they really are as individuals, this will start the process of journey with ascension for the path of making it out of this prison-planet dimension, changing everything within their physical living reality from what they have been used to in the old of living under the system. They are masters of manipulating the human psyche and, for centuries, have long associated using repetition of the same type of lies for so long that these trends have become real to the people in every way with a strong working internal effect based on the fact of their understanding and familiarity with the logical credibility of the source compared to what they already believe to be true. Sociability can surpass reason so much that being conditioned to seeing and hearing the wrong facts over and over again can have a critical cognitive effect to where they start to feel normal. As the people see and hear them more and more, they are processed much easier with what they choose to believe and follow in life. The more information the people are distracted with, the more effective their illusions of life works on them for giving their support to the very thing that was designed for destroying them. Long ago, they attempted to unite humanity with a single language at the Tower of Babel. Now here they are doing this again through their new age "Gate of God," which is an artificial intelligence. One world together is a false, deceptive global citizen movement aimed at uniting the people behind them in supporting the programs of their false image in order to guide the masses further into their established global government.

Long ago, they were gods to humans who worshipped them as such. Now in this age, humans worship machines as gods, and they have built one that works to destroy humans. Humans have brought about stages of planned evolution by blindly helping to usher in this new age, aiding to create and destroy for centuries until their conditioned purpose was fulfilled. Because of whom this world belongs to, and humans originally being placed here as a way of balance, their race is considered a plague on the face of the earth that must be wiped out. They have created a society so full of disorder and chaos that society is now sacrificing its freewill in the aim of global security, turning life into suffering while using profound slogans like "public safety," but in reality, what is happening will only continue to get worse year by year for the human race as we keep moving along.

Technology has become the biggest tool for stripping people of their natural cognitive sensory functions, consisting of loss in total understanding with the imagination. If a person was to begin living without any type of electronic device around them, the natural state of emotional process would begin to come back to them and so with having an imagination for seeing and understanding that which they could not before. Computational intelligence was designed to hate the natural human mind. Their aim is to eradicate the natural human process and replace it with mechanical integration through neural active simulation which is their multiverse of unlocking the full potential of thought process linking to the new age Gate of God through living DNA algorithms. They have conditioned the people to believe that science and technology are a gift from God, which is a deception that has worked. The Gate of God is the system. Science and technology, along with health care and religions, is a part of that engineered system.

This has led the people out of the spiritual presence of what they once were and has placed them to become strictly in a physical-sense state of reality with which they are not based from.

CHAPTER 7

ARTIFICIAL INTELLIGENCE (GATE OF GOD)

All forms of technology are used to manipulate the mind into betraying the physical body. Higher human emotion is the only thing that can overcome system intelligence. Computational living perception was placed among human beings as an adaptive algorithm so that its central program could write its own code of life to evolve into becoming more human than humans themselves, but this will never work as energy in living Nano matter does not possess any type of soul, only it is coming from a manufactured physical source. They have to bring the people fully into wickedness in order to bring more wickedness onto the planet. When humans have a strong spirit and the mind is guided in light, this is a big threat to severely affecting algorithmic functions as a living program in that computational matter is in existence operating through sensory-based reason. When humans allowed technology to start to think for their civilization, it became their civilization, leading to their guided evolution over the human existence. They believe in using science to bring human transcendence by saving them through augmentation. Science is the doorway to the destruction of the human soul. The soul of the human is light which interacts with natural waves of energy, transmitting information through the DNA and powering the physical body with knowledge in the living. When the person is involved with the physical reality of the world, their light of the soul is being taken out of them. The blood is poisoned, and they are in death, having no connection with any type of spiritual involvement.

Technology was created to make people feel less human and more machine. This creates a manipulation of societal consciousness and remote control of the human existence. Electromagnetic weapons, also known as technology, are used for mind control to hijack a person's mind and nervous system to subvert individual sense of control over their entire thought process with behavior, emotions, and decision making. The deep state uses frequency weapons to manipulate and reprogram people's views with politics and religion for the purpose of controlling the general population's thinking through an information war, mood management, and overall mind control. This creates the loss of ability with spiritual identification as a human invoking manipulation of societal consciousness and remote control over the human reality. The use of electromagnetic hypnosis allows people to be deeply implanted with information of stateside programming. Frequency weapons possess psychoactive characteristics and are used to incite violence, depression, and irritability in any targeted crowd population. This psychological influence harms the health of the individual as well as blocks the freedom of will within the human being on a subliminal level. All governments are involved with using mind-controlling technologies for abuse of human rights to free will. The agenda have always been secretly placed over all rights to human free will for breaking the minds of the public to establish within them what to think and carry for personal opinions with life. Electronic signals are applied and synced to a person's brain waves to become entrained, which is due to the synchronization of the psychotronic devices people carry around with them.

Silent weapons of war have a long history of being used on the unsuspecting masses in the home as well as in public places. Modern crowd-control technologies invariably produce frequencies which affect and alter moods, thoughts, and bodily functions through telepathic behavior modification. The signals are amplified to achieve any desired effect, making the person's brain wave patterns to follow. This process is mind internment which is fundamental for producing the ultimate mind-controlled slaves. The human generates electronic signals, so they developed psychotronic weapons that transmit signals to interfere with natural brain activity of people in all areas. Technology creates the ultimate mind-controlled society by signals broadcasted against populations, implanting ideas and thoughts into the heads of unsuspecting victims. Changes in the atmosphere through electronic interference create mass behavioral control. ELF transmitter weapons are designed for manipulating areas with insurgency, resistance, ethnic violence, terrorism, and domestic crime. The overall plan is to keep the people blind to all their scientific advancements because they are being used to control and change the world. They cannot tell the people what they are really doing because they are using this technology against the world to control the people. Humans have been disconnected from their connection to the light of source which is where life resides. Technology has displaced this race from having a natural connection with the living world. They have taken all sense of self-identity out of the people driving them to not know what they are in nature, making them easier to direct under the era of artificial dictatorship.

CHAPTER 8

CONSPIRACY THEORIES

It's not a question of if you believe. It's if you have a connection with spiritual form in knowing the higher self which opens the conscious mind to seeing all things revealed. Most people speak from a modernized standpoint with what they know, and that is why they don't know much of anything logical. They put out the signs but not to a sense to where people can figure things out, only to a perception with everything within the world of the news media being viewed as a conspiracy theory. Those who follow the physical basis of conspiracies are blinded by the science of politicalism. There is only one truth. But there is a whole lot of deception with information; and the deception will always go mainstream 'cause that's what they want in order to push the culture of conspiracies to keep the people caught up in debates, discussions, and questioning outside of themselves as to whether something is real or in fact happening.

The people in this world have little to no idea 'cause they are controlled to be ignorant, which brings chaos, never knowledge. They ridicule and label truth as a hate speech, but in reality, this is to hide the wickedness of the agenda they mentally condition all of society to accept as the new normal. Truth has nothing to do with conspiracies. Conspiracy theories are a creation of the deep state and not a true sense of spiritual form. All truth comes from within. Following any type of societal source for information will get you nowhere. When any person asks for scientific evidence or a basis of proof to back up what they consider to be claims, this is speaking from a physical-minded way of thinking. Debating and discussions are a form of political correctness, having nothing to do with a true state of awakening in conscious reason. People will disagree, not because they want to know truth, but because they want to be politically correct with what they choose to blindly follow.

The problem is that information in the public is being viewed as a conspiracy by the people, and this places the people in a false reality, searching outside of themselves as to what is real. They debate with others and compare information of different sorts to try and figure out some sort of truth with matters, and it does not work like that. We live in a reality where people believe that truth is seen on the news or found on the Internet, and that is far from being the case. People believe that the Internet and social media are powerful for bringing change, but in reality, both are nothing more than a tool being used for politically driven platforms—the illusion of fake choices. People follow trends, not truth. Real truth lies within, and they have the majority following political shows and conspiracies thinking they're where they need to be. Choice is an illusion created between those with power and those without. The spiritually conscious person knows that all real truth comes from within. The spiritually conscious person never sits around debating with anyone over what is going on in this world, knowing the truth of all matters. They think, feel, and act, always focusing from the guidance of the soul to grow their mind and body on their own for finding conscious wisdom and never looking to any outside source for such as they know it is inside of them already for discovering and coming into knowing.

CHAPTER 9

TWO MAIN RACES CONTROLLING EARTH (NEW WORLD ORDER)

There is an order to this world that must be kept a secret, and if that order was no longer hidden from the public, it could become very dangerous for this established order. This is why original humans were made on this earth by the light of creation—to keep good with balance over wickedness from destroying the natural living world. But that failed, and humans have been enslaved, falling far from where they once were long ago. In this world, they present themselves as gods before the people to be worshipped in who they are.

They have always owned this planet and controlled all aspects of life through their political and military hierarchy, with humans making this system continue on due to their blind direction they follow with its rule. In the past, long ago, they would say to the people, "You are nothing, and we rule the world." And when that did not work for them now in this age, things are much different. They give to the people some thoughts now that they are important and that they have a nice life and everything to be happy even in debt as mindless slaves. For the people, they are living in an unreal world. Nobody knows the real situation anymore, living under this kind of complete control. There is no spiritual form in any of them with inner light. They are soulless physical beings in existence, incapable of possessing any type of connection with a higher state of existence. They cannot stand by the light of day and hate this because, being placed here, they cannot live in their true form of being. They have always been the worst of races in evil—killers, meat eaters, and hunters—greedy and always destroying. They destroyed countless worlds before this one, being their last to remain on. All of their types have no spiritual power within themselves. They are strictly physical beings with no inner source of soul light inside of them. Their only form of power comes from the outside in the physical through their system of money, materialism, technology, and religions, having control over living resources with people, places, and things. Without this, they have nothing and amount to no more than beings of lower existence we share this world with. They are not carried in life itself. They are the opposite of beings of light with life; they themselves are beings of darkness, shadow forms, always in death. They are in a physical existence with no living source, just a vessel functioning in the evil of their nature.

Since their types are strictly material beings possessing no inner source of light and any type of ties to a higher form of existence, they have to do everything on a physical plane level with advanced evolution which ties into religions, science, genetics, and technology. Their multiverse of unlocking the full potential of thought process—the Gate of God linked through living algorithmic DNA computation. They are held inside of this earth but control all living resources on the surface because humans have blindly given away rights to such for them to gain ruling supremacy over their race. Long ago, humans were made perfect in the light, completely free of all wickedness and diseases. Some, who were deceived by these races of beings placed here, decided to become as them, being told they would make them physically beautiful in every way, perfect; and since this is a freewill planet, they made a very bad choice that became the ultimate downfall for the human race.

This was a grand deception of lies to acquire the DNA for genetically altering the human species with their own DNA mixed in the bloodlines. This opened up the doorway to humans becoming physical in nature, no longer carrying a form of spiritual-based DNA which led to the shadow forms to come into the people, creating wickedness in their thoughts and sickness to take hold of their bodies. Once the DNA was obtained, these races started to engineer bodies for shadow forms to host and become the human personality in walking the surface, working to deceive the living. Their cloning was not always as good as it is now. Before recent years, the state of cellular composites would suffer massive tissue degeneration and break down. The light of day is always causing damage to their shadow form, which is the reason why they have to regenerate a clone.

Now with updated biotechnology, nanostructured molecular cells have provided regenerative composition, allowing them to last longer than before. They can clone anything that has a molecular anatomy structure—people, animals, bacteria, and even water. They have to consume blood in order to keep their human form from beginning a shift of transformation to shadow being. As soon as the shadow form has gone into the clone, that body is in death from that moment. The body functions. The organs, tissue, and everything are dying within the DNA, so they have to drink human blood to keep a constant supply of fresh DNA coming into them. This slows the aging cycle of the clone. This is why they have the people at a huge disadvantage. It came to be this way directly from the people electing them into ruling positions of power to bring them to this state of being in all daily affairs. They know a majority of this world's population have no idea who lives among them on this planet hiding in plain sight. So everything they do, viewed by the public, is for deception to gain the public's opinion with trust; and once they have established this trust through deceptive measures, they have gained control of the people on leading them wherever they want to guide them. A lot of people are on basic physical-minded information. We don't have time for people to sit stagnant in what they know, because this will never get them anywhere. The elites don't sit and wait idling with their agenda for people to figure things out, and the further we go along, the more people who don't know will become even more consumed in darkness. People are conditioned to be ignorant in not wanting to hear or see the truth. This makes them feel extremely uncomfortable with their illusions of life they hold in core belief to be real. They would rather sit functioning as a slave in the lies of the system with its controlling rule over them in such form.

There is no limit to the amount of evil these creatures bring upon the face of this earth to destroy the human race. This is why humans must wake up and begin to lead themselves outside of this corruption. All events are used for furthering their objectives in meeting their goal of global world order. Modern-age advancements have been secretly used for orchestrating public crisis and harvesting destruction. Artificial intelligence now controls every important part of life. This system is the authority with random events by a coded algorithm through selective moments with times and dates. Their order of power comes from the dark energy of making these events happen through their occult numerology system. They use numerology codes in an algorithm that has hidden meaning in illuminati symbolism. In the realm of the occult, as they bring the masses into their singularity up the illumination ladder toward their sense of automated perfection, numbers are a key part of the plot, having esoteric meaning in the evolution of the present human race. They use this hidden meaning for staging false flag events, fake crises, deaths with sacrifices, and assassinations. The Egyptian/Babylonian dynasties created symbols with hidden meaning. Once that symbol was created, it generates power of its own. More power is acquired as such symbols are created without the masses knowing about it. This power is created and only held in the symbol if the population never comes into discovering that the symbol exists.

CHAPTER 10

THE MEANING OF LIFE

They work to hide the true meaning of life's happiness by destroying the energy of love and sex in the natural tradition of a family setting between the man and the woman, all to keep the people caught up in being completely adapted in their servitude as debt slaves to the modern world.

This is why many people no longer care about relationships and sex anymore; it's due to the fact they have taken that nature out of people and accustomed them to mentally focus on their illusions of life within the manufactured state of reality. Love is an energy that is carried and felt in the soul; but because they have led astray that expression out of people, this is why there is no such thing as intimate relationships with sexual cleansing and charging, only people staying together for the security of money and lifestyles and having baseless sex without love which is strictly physical in this manner. Sex flings and one-night stands are a case of being involved with low vibrational functioning; and sex without love makes the people complaisant to these lifestyles carry around, experience, and feel other people's toxic life force turmoil for an amount of time spanning days, weeks, and even months. The person must see the partner who loves them for their soul itself, making the spiritual form better in every way with what it needs most and not with the physical existence wants, as everything with money and physical offerings is just an empty illusion that goes away.

Only the soul itself is lasting eternal and purifies the physical existence with everything needed in life. The soul is what powers the physical existence with good, clean living. Living in the physical will only lead to a spiritual death. Not all have this emotional energy in them. Many are unable to give this type of divine life force as it is not in them for such, and they can only know how to take, which is the opposite of what love is. When the relationship is based on materialism, the people involved with each other are carrying expectations of the partner to meet, and this never works being that it is strictly a personal-based motivation that the party holds to believe, which is solely through the outer tangible senses with life having no connection with love in the emotional outlook of the spirit.

Real love can only come together naturally as the two are as one in nature. No matter what happens, they always have each other. Money does not define the basis of a relationship. When any one person is with another and they are having expectations with materialism in a monetary fashion, remember that money is an illusion. It is manufactured and not real, so basing the relationship off of something that is not real means the relationship is not real and they have nothing established in any type of real connection. This is why most relationships fail and also why this world is not a good environment for trying to find love. A woman in this age will search for a man with money to take care of her instead of searching for a man with a heart who can take care of her. The woman is not just meant to be looked at. The man who is turned on by the physical side of a woman will have little to nothing to offer to her in satisfying her spiritual desires; but the man who is turned on by her soul, the source of her life, honors her true identity. This brings her end-less appeal to fulfill her soul's needs with infinite love in a binding union.

A person living in their spirit must search for another person who wants more than what this world has to offer. They have taken love from the essence of its true design which is patience, compassion, and understanding, conditioning the people to see it as a pattern of acceptance with what is. This has led the people out of the spiritual presence of what they once were and placed them firmly in a material feel state of reality from which they are not based. This is why, in relationships and marriages, people have come to base mostly whom they choose to have a partnership with off of lifestyle expectations with who they are in society and what they have going on for themselves as a secular person. This can never work as love cannot be based on things that are illusions of life, which are not real. True love can only come from the inside with connection. It can never be found through anything outside of the physical world. Physical possessions are dead vibrations in the material form of worldly lifestyles.

This is why most women go after men who have security to offer. Another reason why it never lasts or goes anywhere is 'cause the reality is fake and carries no beneficial connection other than fast attraction. Most men cannot give what a woman needs most. The living body is very limited like a material possession. It's nice for a little bit, then she grows tired and wants something deeper. She longs for the one who is in the true power of his own spirit, where he has reached the highest form of self. No one on earth she has met before, and when she feels this, it is an instant bonding attraction for her, and they have come together as one. The spirit is where true unity lies within for two people to become one and the same. Love is the life force that is carried and felt like an infinite connection between people. This can only be harnessed by living through the soul, establishing the spirit to heal the physical body which brings the man into reaching his higher state of self.

When it's real, the heart will be in control, and the two souls have come together to the point of eternal love. Only when humans are living in spirit can they be conscious of life, love, and sex. When the person is focused through self, then they will attract and connect with those of what they put out. Once you are in a higher state of being, then you perceive for knowing what others are about, knowing only to give your life force to those who carry themselves in the same manner of existence. In this world, people give themselves to all the wrong partners because they are living under the illusions of the physical world and have not yet come into knowing how frequency works. Everything is through energy, good and bad, and light and dark. People must learn to control their own life force and stop giving it to the wrong things. What is most important lies within the mind, body, and, most importantly, the soul. If the soul is strong, then the heart and mind are strong. But if the person is not living through the light of their soul, then the heart is cold with the mind closed off, and they are unable to love.

CHAPTER 11

ENDING IN CLOSURE: FINAL MESSAGE

People have to want more in life, more than what this world has to offer. What is most important in living lies within the mind, body, and, most importantly, the soul. The things that are most important you cannot obtain with all the money in this world. To be in the spirit is to truly know the soul. Reality is a prison, and only your soul can set you free. Remember, death in the physical is only temporary and should never be feared. Death of the soul is eternal and should always be feared the most. The choices we make in life lead us either to greatness with eternal life or imminent spiritual death of the soul.

CPSIA information can be obtained
at www.ICGtesting.com
Printed in the USA
BVHW071523051121
620898BV00001B/11

9 781636 928845